Nature is better than you and me

A recall to get into Nature's world

Vishal Arun Sheldekar

pencil

ISBN 978-93-5610-375-7
© Vishal Arun Sheldekar 2022
Published in India 2022 by Pencil

Contributors:
Editor: Professor Ram Sir
Editor: Teacher Ms. Rutuja Gaikwad
Editor: Teacher Ms. Teju

A brand of
One Point Six Technologies Pvt. Ltd.
123, Building J2, Shram Seva Premises,
Wadala Truck Terminal, Wadala (E)
Mumbai 400037, Maharashtra, INDIA
E connect@thepencilapp.com
W www.thepencilapp.com

Author biography

This is to the incredible readers who have stumbled upon his stuff in your own precious hands.

Vishal Sheldekar has announced his first Poetry book for Nature. As it is said that, Nature knows its business better than you and me, This book is dedicated to his teacher, Sir Sudhir Shetty and Mrs Joice Fernandes for their excellent teaching in the fields they are.

He continued to be an avid nature reader from his school times. That leisure was precious and spent an inordinate amount of his youth viewing nature. He travelled to various places and saw beautiful sights. He says that half of the world no longer remembers nature in today's fast-growing time.

He had won many certificates for his writings during school and college times. He did his schooling at Sardar Vallabhbhai Patel Vividhlakshmi Vidyalaya and graduated from KES Shroff College of Arts and Commerce. His first poem, "The Hollow Space" had been published in his college magazine. He participated in social service and tree plantations to stop global warming. He also took participation in poetry competitions and his poetry- "Human's Nature" had been selected among the 448 participants from 500 participants conducted by Blooming Kalakar.

Vishal lives in India and the city of Mumbai along with his exceptional perfect blessed mother.

CONTENTS

Nature is better than you and me

I asked God
How does the child learn to see?
says don't ask me, my lord
Nature is better than you and me.

Asked the wings flying in the sky
Why am I not with thee?
From the beak falls message a by,
Nature is better than you and me.

Asked the blossoms at the early dawn
Why is it so winsome during your bloom?
The signal of the flowing breeze passed and said,
Nature is better than you and me.

Asked the Stars and Moon, uplooking the sable black
Why so far from the breathing soul?
Says, we all twinkle on that spot
Nature is better than you and me.

The Flowing River

Out I stepped on the lawn
under the monstrous sky,
For long, I saw the misty dawn
The silent river running by.

The river flows and it smiles
in the blink of my eyes,
From distance to long miles
My gaze will not say lies.

The shining star changed its way
Flashing on the top of the inlet,
Looked like, both made my day
And made me reset.

It travelled and sounded in the burble
Thinking of the thirst in my throat,
Viewing its beauty, have no words verbal
And started to write about her in my note.

Under the Sun

The fair breeze called me
outside under the Sun
On the moss, I sat on my knee,
That silence was full of fun.

The shine was bright
On the leaves, the sea and the sand,
I viewed it through my sight
and slowly blinked down on the land.

Sudden my eyes looked in the east
And it passed with the river,
Made me feel to sing as an artist
My hands started to shiver.

Under the Sun,
I viewed twitter flying ahead of it,
Singing their melodious vocal,
And made me dance to their beat.

The Smiling waves

Giving a smile
to her is my aim.
Stretching all from a mile
and landed with the glowing flame.

It swiftly swept on the sand
and touches over my toes,
Like a child is cuddling in her hand
And felt her love so close.

The poet passes with it,
and withdraws from the sand,
It teaches the human not to quit,
And dropped me back on the land.

Ended the day
and viewed the sundown
Before living, I joined my pray
And left happily seeing the mount.

Diamonds on the leaves

Arose cold weather before the dawn
When some of the ants got a sudden hitch,
Oh! What a terrible breeze passed
And unfurl a frozen climate on the beach.

Neither too late, nor delay it works on time,
with proper skills and thoughts;
A red rose bloomed on the vacant sublime,
On listening to the chirping delightful song.

The dews were shining
through the beam of a glowing star,
Amazed! to view its light
Even I was standing far.

The moment comes to save her life,
was unable to cop up her weight,
Oh! A terrible breeze passed by
By that time it was too late.

The Hollow space

I gazed my eyes under the space
By inhaling fresh breath in a happy mood,
When a murky cloud appeared in that place
A dream came during my childhood.

Besides the bank, beneath the tree
The cold waft passed in a twittering way
Like the cloud's coming down, making us free
Along the margin of a bay.

Before decades, the space was full of twinkles
With no aeroplane and air shuttle;
After decades, it played hide and seek.
Like the child on the ground playing hurdles.

I recognized that it was a rainy day
When suddenly raised dawn,
It was all dark not assuming a day
When thundering voice broke from the hall.

The Sun

My last smile waked a rise,

    Which bloomed from east to west

Then all at once, I viewed its size

     It made me put to test.

Waiting for flies to move and dance,

    Who dives on valves and hills;

And headed up with beauty glance,

    Which made her glad she feels.

The shine then flashed on my eye,

    Who sparkled in the fluttering breeze

And thaught the humans not to lie,

    The difference made me seize.

The Green Grass

The murmuring in the sunlight,

The white foam flew

The lapping of the water

sounded soft in the view.

The horizon spread,

over the mountains and cliff

The double-double double beat played in the leaf.

The flowing waft of the air,

turned the shade green

The sleeping eyes on a rolling mat

sparkled on the screen.

The rise was here,

and the cooling was there

The dew lying on thc grass,

Came across with a little care.

The Sound of air

I awoke before the dawn

Hearing the soothing sound of air,

On hearing the two twitter

Who gathered both in pair.

The funny air flowed

Blowing the saffron leaves of the tree,

It touched me and suddenly I bowed

Making everything free.

It moans round with many voices

And hook the silence of the sleep,

There is anything left with some choices

And an alarm sounded in beep.

Showers on the lawn

Remembering the spring of mist
The star left behind the cloud,
Sudden, the weather turned a twist
The sound of rain patter aloud.
The noise of the thunder,
Awaked me from the dwell
A pinch dropped on my eyelid, I wonder
Like the drizzle on the grass, I fell.

Lonely hearing the wild rain
Falling swiftly on the lawn,
Splashing and dusting on the trees again,
The fresh florals were born.
The water here and the water there
That routed the muddy smell,
It leaps and splat and took care,
When nature rings the bell.

The Down fall

The leisure turned the twist

With no voice of its own

The road is all day forlorn by mist,

And swiftly the breeze had blown.

Hidden the shine,

The lazy clouds gathering by,

The rains going to fall on time

On the thin veil of my eye.

The showers begin to fall

Sweeping the wet smell around,

Though it is, as tiny as small

 Most screaming, some squealing the sound.

Horizon

Long and far I saw a sight
Hiding behind my soul,
The rays sparkled on the carpet so bright
That lighted the colour of the coal.
Headed my walk in that zone
Thanks! The horizon greeted
With a warm gleaming smile alone,
To me, the sea is happily treated.
What can you see?
On the flowing sea and the land
The sun, the twitters chuckles with glee
Listening to the ambient as a band.

Breeze

I stepped on the sand,

And welcomed the warm breeze

It swift from sea to land

Which made me bow on my knee.

The wind barren my thought

And carried me a long way

Both in silence tied the knot,

There were no words to say.

My breath was eddying and dancing

Along with the soft gentle breeze

Long from far, the bird was glancing,

The difference made me seize.

Creepers

I stepped into the nursery
walking on the green moss,
Singing and twittering in the eyries
Without a pause.

It raises tall and thick
holding each other they know,
A beak fall message a by
Like the river, the river should flow.

No one going to break me nor king
I have more length of span,
Rolling up on the wall
It can only be seen in the glen.

It messages humans,
To grow tall and long,
And support each one
Singing a new delightful song.

That Evening

I saved the time

To spend the evening dusk,

Walking, I saw the bloomed flower

Will soon get covered like a husk.

I headed up my eyes to heaven

Seeing the fleet of birds arriving at the nest

The breezy air passes on my face

It made me put to test.

Such a beautiful evening it is,

Hearing the twitters singing the song,

The night is about to come

Which would be as far as long.

The Golden grass

It was much warmth on the lawn,

In the late after twelve noon

There I viewed the tired grass

Of that picture so soon.

Much I've travelled,

in the field of golden grass;

It dances when touches the young feet

Viewing all, with my eyeglass.

I am the gilt,

Which is blessed by the sun

That silent touch

Made me enjoy, made me fun.

The first bloom

The last day dipped so fast

And there rise the early dawn,

I joined the day forgetting the past

And the first bloom was born.

I stopped on the glen

to see the bloom's tragic

As it pulled me deeper,

I saw the flowers' magic.

Then raised the host,

Behind the mount from east,

Flashed on the floret so brightly

It deserves that at least.

The Waterfall

Gurgling between the rocks,

is the brilliant flowing water,

So crystal clear and full of love

is like one little father's daughter.

I scaled on the trekk

And sighed! There was no rise

Only the sound of the whispering fall

is passing through my eyes.

Bubbling full of joy

And gushing through the brook,

And down into the ravine

I jotted it down in the book.

It makes a note to the human

to live the peace of life;

Though it falls on the earth

And flow endlessly to strive.

In the nest

She builds the nest, my darling
on the woods of evergreen,
Some little wren seeks around.
And warble a song in between.

She is hindering here and hindering there
Gathering shreds and threads,
Finding a mate and laying some eggs
And shield it with their sheds.

The baby bird chirps and chirps
Loudly and the mother hears,
And feed them worms
And then after it disappears.

One foggy day drives the rain
And showers little on the lass,
So joyous and gay they were,
It seems the rhythm played in jazz.

Beds of Violets

The sun in the sky

was shining gay,

Scattering its light on the beds, I sighed

That left me to be there and stay.

The valves of beds

All over I see;

The feelings in the heart it spreads,

That rather chuckle with glee.

It's time to awake, she whispered low

I heard walking through,

All are dressed and shining so glow

Said me, it's only for you.

It is the sheet of the bed

Swaying and dancing in my view

And seeks the fragrance on its tiny head,

That stuck and lasted like glue.

The Night Cloth

So quiet after the dusk
I loiter under the sky,
The world is fast asleep
On the pillow where they lie.

Sudden seen the spread of cloth
Left down on the earth,
That evening star does shine
Now is the time for mirth.

It gives the inner peace
Where you and just be you and you
The silent time that is going to come,
Wiggle, wiggle till the moon is blue.

The birds are silent in their nest
And the stars twinkling so,
To keep them all from any harm
To God, I heartedly owe.

Carrying me away

I stamped to set off

Inside your skiff

To skirr the vast ocean,

To raise the sail

And carries me away

In the slow sailing motion.

Up and down, chasing the waves

And getting control of;

To bow the clouds across so high

To the creatures of the deep;

And when the sun is down

The night comes falling from the sky.

In Nature's womb

Anxious, I was the whole day
And true the horror I have seen,
Behold in pain the force
To be in the womb I'm keen.

Lonely, I felt outside still
And no one to cure me,
The sleet of dry leaves spread through the air
And touched the skin of my knee.

Travelled much to be with her
Weeping shed with tears,
And finally was in her womb,
Without any fear.

Holding close and tightened in her arms,
There I inhaled a deep wheeze,
The love, care and the feeling in my heart,
The whole of nature sees.

The White sphere

On my walk, I glimpse the sky

There is a sphere overhead,

And the beauty of the shine

Flashing O'er the small seawater thread.

The moon at night

carries the silence around,

Yet, I stand alone, aloof

Conducting no melodic sound.

It was midnight,

The crescent smiled at me

The owl hoots in the dark,

It is all for the love of thee.

On the sheet of the black

Dazzling and shining brighter and brighter,

Yet you feel how happy I am

Seeing the earth glowing much much whiter.

The Unskipped dawn

I dreamt the last night

keen to see the dawn

Midnight after, I viewed the sight,

Thank God! The last night had gone.

The light glimpsed in the sky

Flashing all over the earth,

To the blooms, rivers and mountains so high

A place where there is no pain of birth.

I might skip all things

Except for the dreams in the dawn,

Seen flying so high to wings,

I made up my mind that I had to go on.

Sky - The Sea

I'm strolling under the sky

Enjoying the lovely breeze

Then suddenly pinched a thought to apply

For making Sky - The Sea.

Hearing the mirage while walking

And gazing at the clear sky

The vision changed from hard to soft

and there I saw those birds fly.

I awe of the whimsical cloth,

which is as soft as fleece;

This blue does not change, still and pale

and gently made a rose peace.

Without the blossoms

While the long dawn is awakening
And the air was blowing a long way,
I can hear its soothing voice
On that beautiful day.

The glorious beautiful pink flowers
 short living a day
and looked so fresh to bloom,
Amazed! It was all on my way.

The absence of blossoms
is like a mother without her child,
The simple grace of her grin
It is much unlike and styled.

The sunrise was at its peak
and is about to glow,
And asked why not blossoms?
Asked then where it will grow.

The Risen Cloth

Up behind the scale,
I saw the fresh dawn in my eyes
The upper rim appears on the horizon,
which brightens the dark and stormy skies.

The gold cloth rises up
and shines on the whole earth,
Its shadow falls on my teacup
My heart was full of mirth.

The skin is so soft, its shimmers
and the sun shines in my wild eye,
Why does the light force me back?
As I viewed it in my sigh.

Glad I was, I told the sun!
In free air and an open glade,
And sheds a warm and glittering look
And shield everyone from the shade.

Colours of Nature

The star hauls up and brightens the earth,

The beauty has so much to say

Every colour in our sigh,

makes the pleasant beautiful day.

Green holds the garden

and highlights the colourful flowers

In another way, seeing the abode of all beasts,

blessed with the wet rainfall showers.

The upright limit is on the top

and the wind blowing on the face,

Viewing the beauty of nature around

Realized! There is no better place.

Lunch with Nature

I raised my eyelids to look around

The beautiful nature blows my mind,

All I set off from the roof

To have lunch with nature made me remind.

Ready to avail my steps

On the lawn quenching my thirst,

The little shades of light reflect the dew

Which gleams in my view at first.

The day has not ended yet

It is just noon,

I'd been all day long and very ravenous

and seat for lunch so soon.

On the river bed

A lot of time spent, in the weald

seeing the lush green view,

Felt to change my mind

And stepped under the blue.

It was all bracing everywhere,

inhaling the fresh blow;

I walked hearing the peaceful sound

And saw the river flowing slow.

Inside I saw,

It was the hollow, the trees and the Sun,

Then I cupped my hands in it

And splashed some, it was fun.

Amazed! I was on the earth,

Looking at this lovely sight

It was so alluring and calm,

That made me quiet.

Until we meet

Even in the darkest days

The sun shines still

Walking for just a little while

With joy, I standstill,

From heart to heart to the nature

Said my thoughts are running for you,

It seems to live through each new day

And express your feelings in my view.

Sometimes the fact when I'm alone

Will always cause me pain;

But our nature stays forever in my heart

Until we meet again.

www.ingramcontent.com/pod-product-compliance
Lightning Source LLC
LaVergne TN
LVHW040045150726
843364LV00038B/1020